사랑의 빛
THE LIGHT OF LOVE

ALSO BY YOON-HO CHO

사랑의 빛
THE LIGHT OF LOVE

Translated into and from Korean by
Eunhwa Choe, Rachel S. Rhee,
Kyung-Nyun Kim Richards,

KEL해외문학사 ¦ CCC 공동출판
Co-Published by
Korean Expatriate Literature
California, USA & Seoul, South Korea
&
Cross-Cultural Communications
New York, USA
2018

Editor/Publisher: Stanley H. Barkan
Cross-Cultural Communications
239 Wynsum Avenue
Merrick, NY 11566-4725/USA
Tel: 516-868-5635 / Fax: 516-379-1901
E-mails: cccpoetry@aol.com/cccbarkan@optonline.net
www.cross-culturalcommunications.com

ISBN 978-0-89304-614-9

Library of Congress Control Number: 2018933190
Korean Bilingual Poetry Series #4
In cooperation with Korean Expatriate Literature

First printing of Bilingual Edition: June 2018

Printed by Changjo Munhak
86 Gajwaro, Seodaemun-gu,
Dongchun Academy # 5th
Seoul, Korea
Tel: 02-374-9011
E-mail: hmpo@hanmail.net

Cover art: *Cold Waters*, acrylic on canvas, 15 x 15″, 2001 by Mia Barkan Clarke

Many of the poems in this book have been published in the following books and journals:

Cho, Yoon-Ho & Barkan, Stanley H. (Eds.). *Bridging the Waters: An International Bilingual Poetry Anthology (Korean, American, Other).*
(Merrick, NY : Cross-Cultural Communications & Korean Expatriate Literature, 2013)
Lips, 2011(New Jersey Poetry Magazine)
Confesiuni, 2015 (Romanian Literary Magazine)
Convorbiri Literare, January Issue, 2015 (Romanian Literary Magazine)
Cyclamens and Swords, April Issue, 2014 (Israeli Literary Web-based Journal)
Paterson Literary Review, New Jersey, U.S.A. Issues #39 2011-2012.
The Seventh Quarry, Swansea Wales Poetry Magazine. Issue #13, Special Edition, Issues #14 and #15.
Romanian Literary Poetry Magazine, 2017.
Italy E-Book, 2017.
KrytykaLiteracka, 2016 and 2017. (Polish Arts and Letters Quarterly)

|시인의 말|

이제 내가 시집을 내려고 하니 마음이 설렌다.

풀 한 포기 없는 사막과 같은 이민의 삶 속에서 자칫 실망하고 좌절하기 쉽지만, 이 어려움을 극복하는 힘은 곧 사랑밖에 없다. 그래서 사랑을 주제로 한 시를 담으려 노력했다.

특히 내 시들은 내 인생의 여러 가지 문제들을 다룬 인생 성찰의 시를 그려보았다.

이 시집을 미국 출판사와 공동으로 출판해 준 스탠리 H. 발칸(Stanley H. Barkan) 시인에게 감사드린다. 스탠리 시인은 뉴욕에서 도서출판 Cross-Cultural Communications사 대표이며 한국시문학의 세계화에 큰 기여를 하고 있다.

이 시집을 영어로 번역해 주신 김경년 시인 (Kyung-Nyun Kim Richards)님과 이승은 (Rachel S. Rhee) 시인, 그리고 최은화(Eunhwa Choe) 번역가에게 감사드린다.

이 책에 수록된 다수의 작품들은 다음의 책 또는 잡지에 게재됐음을 밝혀둔다.

2018년 봄

—조윤호

As I am about to publish a new collection of my poems, I feel a little anxious and excited at the same time.

In an immigrant life that is as barren as a desert where not a single blade of grass grows, it is often easy to be disappointed and discouraged. The only source of power that helps me to overcome this is love. The poems gathered here are based on the theme of love.

The poems are an effort to reflect on my life laden with problems and issues.

I would like to thank Stanley H. Barkan for co-publishing this collection of poems. Barkan, also a poet, is the president of Cross-Cultural Communications, New York, and a leading contributor in globalization of Korean poetry.

I would like to thank the poets Kyung-Nyun Kim Richards and Rachel S. Rhee and the translator Eunhwa Choe for translating my poetry into English.

Many of the poems in this collection have been published in other previously published other books and journals.

Spring 2018
—Yoon-Ho Cho

차례
CONTENTS

2. ON THIN ICE 살얼음판에서

Part 1
사랑의 빛
THE LIGHT OF LOVE

가을바람

가을바람이 불어오니
내 집 앞에 서있는 나뭇가지에서
낙엽이 진다.

가을바람은
나에게도 다가오더니
유혹하네.
이제 저승으로 가는 게 어떠냐고.

그때 나는 대답했네.
시 쓸 게 너무 많으니
조금만 더 기다려 달라고.

가을바람은
속는 걸 알면서도
고개만 흔들다가 그냥 돌아가네.

THE AUTUMN WIND

The autumn wind blows.
From branches in front of my house
Fallen leaves.

Autumn wind
It came to me
It's tempting.
"How about going to the next world?"

Then I answered.
"There' s too much poetry to write.
Wait a little longer."

The autumn wind knows
that you are deceiving,
but it shakes its head
and it just goes away.

가을 하늘엔 별이 빛나네

무거운 짐을 내려놓겠다고
나무는 해마다 가을을 불러왔지.

높은 나뭇가지에 있는 잎사귀나
낮은 곳에 있는 잎사귀도
가을은 공평하게 내려놓네.

나도 헛된 꿈들을 모두 내려놓으니
잎이 진 나뭇가지 위에
사과가 익어 가듯

내 마음도
붉게 익어가고
가을 하늘엔 별이 빛나네.

THE STARS SHINE IN THE AUTUMN SKY

To unburden its heavy load
the tree calls for the autumn every year.

The leaves at the top branches
and the leaves at the bottom,
autumn equally sheds them.

As I unload all the empty dreams
like the apples ripening
on the leaf-less branches

My heart also
ripens in crimson and
the stars shine in the autumn sky.

달의 미소

달을 보고 싶으면
나는 밤에 일어나야 한다.
캄캄해야 큰 달을 볼 수 있으니까.

우울하고 싶으면
구름을 불러온 달을 보아야 한다.

나는 밤에 일어나 달을 보아야 한다.
달은 내가 웃을 때마다
미소 지어 주니까.

SMILE OF THE MOON

To see the moon
I need to get up during the night.
Since the big moon can only be seen in the darkness.

To feel depressed
I have to see the moon that brought the clouds.

I have to wake up at night to see the moon.
Because whenever I laugh
the moon smiles.

벌들과의 전쟁

벌은 새벽부터 일어나
부지런히 이 꽃 저 꽃을 옮겨 다니고
벌이 모은 꽃가루는 꿀이 된다.
전쟁을 준비하는 사람들은
수많은 벌을 한꺼번에 죽일
미사일, 핵폭탄을 만들어 좋아한다.
벌이 몰살당했다고
깃발만 나부끼는 승리의 전쟁터
벌과의 전쟁에서 이기면 무엇을 하는가.
벌이 묻혀주는 꽃가루가 없다면
열매 없는 자연은
과연 무엇으로 수확할 것인가.
전쟁광들은
이와 같이 헛된 일만 하니
사람들이 벌보다 나은 것이 무엇인가.

AT WAR WITH THE BEES

Bees are up at dawn
diligently flying from one flower to another
gathering pollen to become honey.

People who prepare for wars
enjoy creating missiles, nuclear bombs
which will kill many bees at once.

Upon exterminating the bees
flying the flag of victory at the war front
what good is it to win the war against the bees?

Without the pollen on the bees
nature will be without fruit-
how would it harvest then?

When the warmongers
only work on futility
how can humans be better like than the bees?

소나기 소리

자갈 밟는 소리 내며
그대 창문 앞에 서니
하늘이 무너지는 소리가 들린다.

번개와 천둥이 치더니
갑자기 소나기 쏟아지는
소리가 들린다.

그 소린
안타까이 그대 마음을 부수고 싶은
내 심장이 뛰는 소리 아닌가.

SOUND OF RAIN SHOWER

With the sound of stepped-on gravel,
as I stand before your window,
I could hear the sound of the caving sky.

After the crack of lightning and thunder,
the sudden sound comes
of pouring rain.

That sound,
isn't it of my beating heart
anxiously wanting the break of your heart?

한 그루 겨울나무같이

무거운 짐을 다 내려놓고
언 땅에 겨울나무같이
너는 맨발로 서 있었느냐?

너는 바람에 흔들리고
비에 젖고
휘날리는 눈보라를 맞아보았느냐?

나무는
다 그렇게 견디어 냈나니.

봄이 오면 언 땅은
겨울을 견디어 낸 겨울나무를 보고
봄볕을 불러들인다.

LIKE A WINTER TREE

After unloading the heavy burden,
like a winter tree on a frozen land,
did you stand there without shoes?

Have you ever been shaken by the wind
and drenched by the rain
and bombarded by the swirling snow?

The tree
has endured all that and more.

When the spring comes, the frozen land
will look at the winter tree that survived the winter
and call in the spring sunshine.

바닷길

푸른 바닷길,
바다 위를 두리번거리고 서서
어느 한 방향을 오랫동안 바라보았다.

숲이나
나뭇잎 떨어진 흔적조차 없고
눈에 보이는 것이란
망망대해 뿐.

그리고 수만 개의 바닷길 앞에서
앞으로 나아가야 할 길을 몰라
밤하늘의 별빛을 보고 나의 길을 택했다.

작은 배 한 척 타고
태풍이 불어오더라도
나는 오늘도 앞만 보고 가는데

갈매기들만 하늘 높이 날아오를 뿐
그러나 돌아갈 길은 보이지 않았다.

SEA ROAD

Blue sea road,
standing by the sea,
I looked in one direction for a long time.

Forest,
there are no signs of falling leaves.
What is visible
is only the boundless expanse of water.

And in front of tens of thousands of seas
I do not know the way.
I saw my starlight in the night sky and chose my path.

Take a little boat
even if a typhoon blows
I am going forward to today.

Only seagulls flying high above the sky
but I did not see the way back.

런던 공원에서

런던의 한 공원,
한 쌍의 오리를 다시 생각 하련다.

수컷 오리는
암컷 오리에게 달려오더니
잔디 속에서 잡은 먹이를 입에 넣어준다.

암컷 오리는
먹이를 먹으면서
달콤한 기쁨을 맛보았겠지.

다툼이 없는 두 마리 오리처럼
나도 행복을 만들어 가리.

AT LONDON PARK

At a park in London,
I recall a pair of ducks.

A male duck rushes to a female duck
to feed her in her mouth
the bait taken from the grass.

I guess the female duck
feels a sweet happiness
when she eats the bait
received from her mate.

Like the pair of ducks
who never had a quarrel,
I want to build our happiness.

두루미의 침묵

독수리가 기다리는 산
깊은 밤하늘의 고요 속에서
소리를 죽이려고
입에 돌을 물고 날아가는
두루미.

저 밤하늘에 죽음을 피해
나 또한 소리 내지 않고
고통의 산을 넘어서 가리.
침묵하는 두루미같이

낮이나 밤이나
입에는 돌을 물고
함부로 쏟아내는 말 한마디
침묵으로 채워 가리.

THE SILENCE OF THE CRANE

The mountain where an eagle awaits.
the crane flies with a pebble in its beak
to muffle sound
within the stillness of the deep night sky.

Making no noise,
I will avoid the death of the night sky
and crossover the mountain of suffering
like the silent crane.

Night and day,
I will hold a pebble in my mouth
and fill with silence
the careless words that pour out.

사랑의 빛

하늘은 높다.
이보다 더 높은 것은
없을까?

바다는 넓다.
이보다 더 넓은 것은
없을까?

이보다 더 높고
이보다 더 넓은 것은
당신 마음속에 있는 빛뿐.

빛이 빛나지 않으면 빛이 아니다.
이 세상을 비추고도
남을 만한 큰 사랑의 빛.

THE LIGHT OF LOVE

High is the sky.
Could there be anything
higher?
Wide is the sea.
Could there be anything
wider?

That which is higher
and that which is wider
is the light in your heart.

Light is not light if it fails to illumine.
The light of great love
vast enough to illumine the world and more.

꽃에서 꽃으로

펄럭펄럭
날아온 나비 한 마리
내게 무엇이 있는 듯이

가장 두렵다는
거센 강풍을 피한
저 작은 날갯짓…

조심스럽게 천천히
마지막이 될지도 모르는
소나기도 지나온 날갯짓…

내게 찾아온 이유는 무엇일까—
나는 두리번거리며 돌아보아도
아무것도 보이지 않는다.

내 마음 속에 핀
작고 노란 꽃을 찾아서
그 먼 길을 펄럭펄럭 날아왔네.

FROM FLOWER TO FLOWER

Fluttering,
a butterfly flew
over me as if I had something.

The fluttering of small wings
that had escaped a most fearsome
bluster.

Gingerly and slowly,
the gestures of the wings
had passed through the rain showers
that might have been their last.

What could be the reason
it had come over to me?
I looked around but
could not see anything.

It had flown over from far off
fluttering its wings
on the look-out for the small yellow flower
that bloomed in my heart.

물처럼

동굴 속에서 떨어지는
한 방울
두 방울의 물.

단단하고 강한 바위 위에도
구멍을 뚫는
물방울

무엇이 약하고
무엇이 강한가?

나도 물처럼
부드러움이 강함을 이기고
단단함을 이긴다는 것을 보여 주리.

LIKE WATER

One drop
two drops of water
falling in a cave.

Water drops
wear out a hole
even on strong, firm rock.

What is weak
and what is strong?

Like water, I too, shall show that
softness wins over strength
and conquers toughness

당신은 어느 쪽인가

내가 어릴 때는
꽃의 아름다움에 취해서
사랑만 있으면
행복 하리라 믿었다.

내가 중년이 되니
꽃은 보이지 않고
돈만 있으면
행복 하리라 믿었다.

이제 내가 늙어
꽃이 시들고 보니
꽃을 사랑하는 마음만 있으면
가장 행복 하리라 믿게 되었다.

WHAT ABOUT YOU?

What about you?

When I was young,
drunk on the beauty of flowers,
I believed I would be happy
if I had love.

In my middle age
I did not see the flowers
and believed that I would be happy
if I had money.

Now that I am old
and the flowers have wilted,
I have come to believe that I would be happy
if only I had heart enough to love flowers.

나비가 가는 길

세상에 많은 길 중에도
나비가 가는 길이 좋아
나는 이 길을 따라 가리.

세상에 많은 길 중에도
나비는 꽃만 찾아 가는 길이니
그보다 더 좋은 길은 없겠지.

나비가 가는 길이라 해도
소나기를 피할 수는 없겠지.

향기는 사람들에게 주고
아름다운 색깔과 꽃잎만 좋아하는
나비가 나는 좋아.

펄럭펄럭 날갯짓하는
나비가 가는 길이
사람들에게 희망을 주기에

WHERE BUTTERFLIES GO

Among the many roads in the world
I like the roads where butterflies travel.
So I will follow one.

Among the many roads in the world
butterflies go only to find flowers.
No road could be better than this.

Even the roads where butterflies travel
cannot avoid showers.

Leaving fragrances to people,
butterflies follow only after the beautiful
colors of the flower petals.
I like that.

The paths fluttering butterflies travel
give us humans hope.

꽃

꽃은
이 세상에서
웃기 위해
피어난다.

나는
당신이 웃는 것
보기 위해
이 꽃을 준다.

FLOWER

Flowers
bloom
in this world
to laugh.

I
give
this flower
to see you laughing.

돌

깨어져도 아픔이 없는
돌이 되고 싶겠지.

홀로 나뒹굴어도 외로움이 없고
헤어져도 그리움이 없는
돌.

죽어도 슬픔이 없는
돌이 되고 싶겠지.

돌은 알고 있으나
대답하지 않는다.

A STONE

A desire to be a stone,
that doesn't feel the pain when it breaks.

No loneliness even when tumbling on its own,
and no yearning even when separated,
that is a stone.

A desire to be a stone,
that has no grief even in death.

A stone knows
but does not answer.

빈 배

강가에 매단 빈 배를 타고
나는 세상 강을 건너가네.

너무 가벼워서
하늘도 날아다니고

배끼리 부딪쳐도
상처 주는 일 없고

이보다 더 좋은 배가
세상에 없으니

그대가 준 빈 배를 타고
오늘도 나는 강을 건너고 있다.

EMPTY BOAT

On the empty boat moored to the riverside
I cross the river of the world

So light
it flies around the sky

and even if boats collide
nobody gets hurt

No other boat
as good as this in the world

Riding the empty boat you gave me
today, too, I cross the river

Part 2
살얼음판에서
ON THIN ICE

눈 위의 발자국

지난겨울 밤
내린 눈으로
세상이 하얗다.
눈 위에 새겨진
두 개의 발자국.
내 집에서부터 시작하여
당신 창문 앞까지
찍혀 있다.
당신이 문 열어주지 않는다면
아픈 내 발자국이 녹아서
강물이 되어 흘러가리.

FOOTPRINTS ON THE SNOW

The world is white
due to last night' s
fallen snow.
Two footprints
on the snow.
imprinted
from my house
to beneath your window.
If you don't open the door
my aching footprints will melt
and flow as a river.

행복이 무엇이냐 하면

나무들이 보여주는 행복이란
내가 세상에서 찾던 것과 다르네.

나는 큰 꽃잎으로
화려한 집을 짓는 것이었네.

하지만 나무가 보여주는 것이란
봄날에 핀 작은 꽃잎들과
그 꽃들이 불러들인 나비들 뿐.

나는 깨달았네.
행복이란 무엇이냐 하면
날 사랑하는 이와 작은 미소를 나누고

겨울 풀잎처럼 낮아져서
한 마디 따듯한 말로
아름다움을 채우는 것이었네.

WHAT HAPPINESS IS

The happiness that trees show
is different from the kind I sought in the world.

Mine was to build an opulent house
with large flower petals.

But the happiness shown by trees
is small blossoms in the spring
and the butterflies attracted to them.

Then I understood.
Happiness is
exchanging small smiles with the one I love,

lowering myself like the winter grass,
and filling beauty
with warm words.

눈 속에서

세상을 뒤덮은 하얀 눈
부드럽고 아름답네.

부드럽다고 눈을
함부로 밟지 마라.

밟으면 밟을수록
칼날이 되는 눈.

부드러운 눈은 쌓이고 쌓이면
큰 나뭇가지도 부러뜨리지.

하지만 내 마음에 사랑이 쌓이면
무겁게 쌓인 눈도 가벼워지네.

IN THE SNOW

The white snow covering the world
is soft and beautiful.

Don't step carelessly on the snow
just because it's soft.

The more it's stepped on
the more snow becomes like ice.

When piled up, the soft snow
even breaks a large branch.

But when love piles up in my heart
even heavy snow becomes light.

거리의 등불

환한 대낮에
등불을 들고 가는 사람,
모두 맹인은 아니다.

비는 오지 않고
구름 한 점 없는
하늘인데…….

화약 냄새로 공기가 탁한 세상은
두려움에 떨고 있네.

캄캄한 세상을 밝히려고
등불을 들고 가는 사람이 있다.
작은 반딧불처럼

나 또한 대낮인데도
등불을 들고 걸어가야 하리.

LAMPLIGHT

People who carry lamps
in broad daylight
cannot all be blind.

It is not raining
and not a single shred of cloud
hangs in the sky.

The world filled with the thick smell of gunpowder
is trembling with fear.

There are those who carry a lamp
in order to light up the world
like a little firefly.

I, too, in broad daylight
must walk carrying a lamp.

살얼음판에서

조심스럽게 겁을 내면서
난 살얼음판 위를 걸었지.

어둠을 밝히는 별 하나
친구처럼 비추는 밤에

얼음이 깨어져
물에 **빠져** 마지막 날이 될 것을
두려워하기보다 나는 뛰었네.

큰 꿈을 바라고
조각난 얼음도
클수록 좋을 것이라 여기면서.

ON THIN ICE

Gingerly and fearfully
I walked on thin ice.

In the night when a lone star
shining in the dark
shone like a friend,

Rather than filled with terror of the ice breaking
and my falling into the water
to meet my last moment,
I ran.

Hoping for a big dream
thinking even the broken pieces of ice
would be better if they were larger.

새 민들레

긴 겨울의 끝
내
뒤뜰에
새 얼굴을 보여주네.

상처받은 마음을 지우고
해마다 피어나는
새 민들레.

나도 이 민들레처럼
지난 해 받은 상처를 땅에 묻고
새 모습을 보여주고 싶네.

FRESH NEW DANDELIONS

At the end of a long winter
they show their fresh new faces
in my backyard.

Erasing all the hurt in their hearts
dandelions bloom anew
each year.

Perhaps I too, like the dandelions,
wish I could bury all my wounds of last year
and show a new face.

기다림

마음이 흔들리는 날은
키 큰 자작나무에게로 간다.

바람이 불면
나무는 흔들렸지.

비가 뿌리면
나무는 온몸에 비를 맞았지.

눈이 내리면
눈을 털며 기다리는 나무가 되었다.

저 끈질긴 나무의 기다림
키 큰 자작나무는 나를 일으켜 세운다.

WAITING

On days when my heart stirs
I go to the tall white birch tree.

When the wind blows
the tree shakes.

When it showers,
the tree is soaked, all over.

When snow comes
the tree turns to a waiting tree
that shakes off the snow.

The waiting of the enduring tree
the tall white birch makes me stand tall.

붉은 겨울 달

당신은
나뭇가지 끝에 걸려 있는
붉은 겨울 달.

빛마저 얼어 있어
내가 안아주고 싶은
얼굴.

구름이 얼굴을 가리려 해도
내 꿈은 변치 않아
부드럽게 다시 차오르는 달빛.

나뭇잎이 떨어진
그대의 발밑에서도
내 영혼은 빛으로 붉게 물이 든다.

RED WINTER MOON

You are
a red winter moon
hanging on the tip of a branch,

the face
that I want to embrace
for even light has frozen.

Though clouds try to cover your face
my dreams have not changed
so the moonlight softly rises again.

My soul is dyed red with light
even beneath your feet
where leaves have fallen

가을 나뭇잎

나뭇잎이 노랗게 물들어
바람에 떨어지고
어디선가 들려오는 소리
그 사람의 발자국소리같이 들리네.

하늘이 투명해서 높아가고
흰 구름도 슬픈 표정을 짓는
가을날
그 사람이 그리워진다.

고요한 밤마다 울어대는
귀뚜라미 소리에
잠 못 드는 밤
그 사람의 가슴에 안기고 싶다.

AUTUMN LEAF

Leaves change to yellow
and fall in the wind.
A sound from somewhere
sounds like that person's steps.

On autumn days
when the sky becomes clear and high
and white clouds look sad,
I miss that person.

On quiet nights
when I cannot sleep
because crickets disturb the peace,
I want to be held by that person.

안개꽃 연가

내 방안에서 화사하게 피어
내 눈을 사로잡은
하얀 안개꽃 한 다발 보았네.

스스로 낮아져서
장미와
카네이션과 튤립과도 어울리는
신비한 꽃.

아무 욕심도 없이
당신을 닮아
희망을 뿌려주는 꽃향기.

다 내어주고도 기뻐하는
안개꽃 한 다발 되고 싶다.
내 어머니 같은

LOVE SONG FOR BABY'S BREATH

A bouquet of white baby's breath
in bright bloom caught my eye
in my room.

Choosing to be humble
to go with roses, carnations,
and tulips . . .
baby's breaths are mysterious flowers.

Having no greed,
like you,
they exude a fragrance
that gives us hope.

I want to be a bundle
of baby's breaths
that rejoice in giving everything
they have,
like . . . my mother.

연꽃

연꽃은 진흙탕에서
온몸으로 젖으며
하나, 둘 연꽃이 핀다.

비 오고
바람 불어도 꺾이지 않고
고개를 꼿꼿이 세우더니

벼랑 끝에 선
뭇 인간들
붙잡아 주려고

어둠이 가득 찬 세상에
사랑은 남는 것이라고
연꽃은 행복한 노래를 부른다.

LOTUS BLOSSOMS

Lotus blossoms bloom
one, two, in the mud
getting wet all over.

Even when it was raining
and windy, they do not break off
but keep their necks straight.

To hold up the many
human beings who are standing
at the edge of the cliff,

In a world that is filled with darkness
only love remains
the lotus blossoms sing a happy song.

복숭아

내 사랑은
6월에 먹는
복숭아 같다고나 할까.

처음 보기엔 복숭아의
그 빛깔이 붉고 강렬한 적황색
식욕은 왕성하지만 딱딱하지.

냉장고에 넣어두고 기다리면
말랑말랑하고
달콤하지.

마지막 여름이 물러가고 나면
내 사랑도 떠나가리.
복숭아의 향기만 남긴 채.

PEACHES

Should I say that my love is
like the peaches you eat
in June?

At first, the peaches are red and are
intense reddish-yellow.
They inspire great appetite but are hard.

You put them in the refrigerator
and wait,
they turn soft and get sweet.

When the last days of summer are over
my love will also depart,
leaving only the fragrance of peaches.

하나의 길

아무리 어려운 일이 생겨도
방황하지 않는다.
꿈이란 헛될 수도 있지만
나무는 하나의 길에 끝까지 매달린다.

비가 내려 캄캄할 때
눈이 보이지 않을 수도 있다.
눈이 내려 온몸이 얼어붙을 수도 있다.
하지만 잠시 후 비나 눈은 떠나고 만다.

나 또한 하나의 길만 보고
날마다 황홀한 꿈을 꾸며
고개를 빳빳이 세우고
끝까지 달려가는 나무처럼 살아가리.

ONE PATH

No matter how difficult something is
it does not wander.
Dreams may be vain
but a tree will stick to one path.

When rain covers the sky in darkness
eyes cannot see.
Bodies may freeze in the snow.
But the rain and snow will soon depart.

Like a tree that lasts till the end
looking at one path only,
dreaming every day most marvelous dreams,
holding its neck straight,
I, too, will live like a tree.

만일 바람이 불지 않는다면

사막에서도
눈이 내리면
무릎 꿇은 들풀들을 본다.

겨울바람이 불면
낮아지고 더 낮아지며
겨울 햇볕으로도
견디어 내는 풀뿌리.

봄바람 불어오니
무릎 꿇은 들풀들,
고요 속에서 깨어나
다시 무성한 풀숲을 이룬다.
만일 바람이 불지 않는다면

IF THE WIND DOES NOT BLOW

Even in the desert,
when it snows,
the grass in the field kneels down.

When the winter-wind howls,
the grassroots grow deeper and deeper
and the grass perseveres in the winter sun.

When the spring breezes blow
the prostrated grass
wakes up in quietude
and builds another lush grass forest.

If it does not give in . . .

소나기

봄바람이 땅 속에서
꽃들을 들어 올리지.

사랑이 오지 않고
소나기가 내린다면
이 꽃과 잎들이 상처만 남지 않겠나.

만일 사랑이 온다면
소나기가 내려서
꽃들이 상처만 남는다 해도
무슨 아픔이 되겠나.

SHOWER

Spring breezes raise up
grass flowers
from the ground.

If love has not come
but only showers,
do nothing but wounds remain
in these flowers and leaves?

If love came,
even if showers inflicted
the flowers with wounds
they would not feel the hurt.

봄비

당신은 봄비
나는
작은 풀꽃

겨울잠에서 뿌리를 깨우느라
지난밤에 봄비가 내렸네.

초록의 새 옷을 입히려
봄비는 잠도 자지 않았나 싶다.

이 비 그치면
찬란한 햇빛 머금고
영롱하게

나는 밝은 모습으로
풀꽃 하나 피워
당신과 함께 숲 속으로 가리라.

SPRING RAIN

You are spring rain
I a small flower in the grass.

Rain was pouring down last night,
to awaken roots from their winter sleep.

The spring rain did not sleep
so that it can put on a new garment of green.

When the rain stops,
I will fill my mouth full of glorious sunlight
most iridescent.

With a grass flower blooming
on my bright face,
I will go into the forest
with you.

달맞이꽃

아메리카의 보름달은 밝네.

나는 보름달이 되고 싶네.
내 어머니의 눈동자같이
밝은

아메리카의 밤하늘에 빛나며
어두운 세상을 밝힐 때

밤마다 나를 바라볼 거야.
내 누이의 얼굴같이
작고 소박한 달맞이꽃은

EVENING PRIMROSE

Oh, how bright the full moon is in America!

I wish I could be a full moon.
bright
like my mother's eyes,

Shining in the night sky of America
and shedding light on a dark world

It will look up at me every night,
the small and simple evening primrose,
like my sister's face . . .

Part 3
바닷가에서
AT THE BEACH

상처받은 꽃

마음속에 상처 한 번쯤
받지 않은 사람이 있을까.

세상에서 가장 아름다운 꽃들도
상처 받으며 피었고
상처 받은 꽃은
사랑하는 길을 찾았지

마음속에 눈물 한 번쯤
흘리지 않은 사람이 있을까.

세상에서 가장 아름다운 꽃들도
눈물 흘리며 피었고
눈물 흘린 꽃은
사랑하는 삶을 깨달았지.

WOUNDED FLOWERS

Can there be anyone
who has never been hurt in his heart?

The most beautiful flowers of the world
bloom with wounds
and such wounded flowers look for
a road to love.

Can there be anyone
who has never shed tears in his heart?

The most beautiful flowers of world
bloomed shedding tears
and flowers that shed tears
understand the life of love.

풀꽃

나는 한 마리 벌입니다.
당신은 풀꽃인가요?
내 가던 길
멈추게 하는 풀꽃 하나.

얼마나 행복할까요,
들길을 헤매다
마침내 풀꽃 하나 찾았으니까.

비로소
나는 깨달았습니다.
풀꽃 앞에 서서
내가 존재하는 이유를
알았으니까.

GRASS FLOWER

I am merely a bee
and you a grass flower?
A flower that stops me
on my journey.

How happy I am
finally to find a grass flower
while wandering through all the fields,

to understand at last
the reason why I exist
before a grass flower.

그대는 꽃이다

그대는 꽃이다.
꽃을 보고 있는 것과 같이
그대는 무지개다.
무지개를 보고 있는 것과 같이
그대는 소나기다.
소나기를 맞고 있는 것처럼
그대는 눈송이다.
눈송이를 맞고 있는 것처럼
그렇다.
사랑은 아름다움을 그냥 보고
맞는 것이기에

YOU ARE LOVE

You are a flower
Like looking upon a flower.
You are a rainbow
Like looking upon a rainbow.
You are a sudden rain shower
Like being drenched by a sudden shower.
You are a snowflake
Like being inundated by snowflakes.
Yes.
Love is just looking at and taking in
Something beautiful.

잠시 후엔

빨갛게 물든 나뭇잎이
가을바람에 떨어지듯이
잠시 후면 너는 떨어질 것이다.

그것을 알면 너는
모른 척 하지만 말고
미리 준비를 해 두자.

늙어간다는 것에도
아름다움이 있고
기쁨이 있지.

나이가 들어도
이웃에게 한 번 더 웃어주고
무거운 짐은 같이 들어줄 수 있는 거야.

붉게 물든 나뭇잎이 떨어지더라도
이런 작은 것들이 행복을 주는 것이니
아름다움이 아니겠는가.

SOON AFTER

As crimson infused leaves
fall with the autumn breeze,
soon after you will fall.

If you know thus,
do not ignore it,
but get ready already.

Even in aging,
there's beauty and
also joy.

Even as we get older,
we could smile once more to the neighbors
and share in carrying the heavy burden.

Even when crimson infused leaves fall,
these small things give happiness
and isn't that in itself a beauty?

길 잃은 양

길 잃은 어린 양 한 마리 만나
그냥 지나치지 않고
돌 봐 준다면
이 세상은 밝지 아니할까?

양이 살던 우리 안으로
길을 안내해 준다면
이 세상은 더 밝지 아니할까?

길 잃은 어린 양의 아픔을
나의 아픔으로 여기고,

어린 양의 고통을
나의 고통으로 느낄 수 있다면
기적이 일어나지 아니할까?

A LOST SHEEP

If you happened upon a lost sheep
and took care of it and not just
pass it by,
wouldn't that make this world a brighter place?

If you led it back
to its old fold,
wouldn't that make this world a brighter place?

If we could take the hurt of a young lost sheep as our own
hurt,
if we could feel the pain of a young lost sheep as our own,
wouldn't that be a miracle?

해바라기 연가

여름날에도 해만 바라보고 키운
꿈이 있었기에
해바라기는 더워할 줄 몰라요.

사랑의 말에 귀 기울이다
훌쩍 키가 큰 당신,
당신 없인 사랑의 말 나는 몰라요.

이웃과 사랑 나누다가
어느새 기쁨이 쌓여
노랗게 물드는 큰 꽃잎.

가을 들녘에 서서
해바라기를 보았어요.
그리움이 자라서 남긴 까만 씨앗들.

A LOVE SONG FOR SUNFLOWERS

Because their dreams were nurtured
while gazing at the sun,
sunflowers do not feel the heat of summer.

While listening to words of love
you suddenly grew tall.
Without you, I would not know the language of love.

While sharing love with a neighbor
your large petals turn to the yellow
of the joy that enwraps you.

Standing in an autumn field
I saw sunflowers.
The black seeds remain,
grown out of longing.

가정이란 작은 천국

가정이란 작은 천국
두 사람이 짊어져야 할 짐이 아니라
서로 미소 짓고
한 마디 따뜻한 위로의 말로
채워지는 아름다움이네.

봄날은 하늘이 맑게 개어 있지만
짓궂은 봄비가 내리듯
서로의 얼굴에
가끔은 눈물 흘리기도 하지.

하늘에 낀 구름도
오래 머물지 못하고 바람에 밀려가니
비 온 뒤 땅이 굳어지듯
마침내 우리의 사랑은
더욱 숲이 무성해 지리.

THE SMALL HEAVEN CALLED FAMILY

The small heaven called family
is not a load to be born by two people.
It is a beauty filled with the
the smiling of one to one another
and with warm words of comfort.

Spring days have clear skies
but naughty spring showers fall.
Some tears do flow
down our faces.

As clouds in the sky
can't stay long before being pushed away by the wind
and as the ground becomes firm after a rain,
our love, too, will at last
grow, a thicker forest.

마음의 냄새

냄새가 나면
나는 그 냄새를 피해 달아난다.
시간과 공간을 지나고
마음의 터널을 지나
멀리 달아난다.

하지만 사람마다
독특한 마음의 냄새를 풍긴다.
슬픈 사람은 눈물 냄새,
행복한 사람은 기뻐하는 냄새,
이기적인 사람은 욕심 냄새…

아무리 도망가도
그 마음의 냄새는
내 곁에서 떠나지 않는다.

SCENT OF THE HEART

When I smell an odor
I run away to avoid it.
I run far away
passing through time and space
and the tunnel of minds.

But everyone has their unique
scent of heart.
The smell of tears from a sad person.
The smell of joy from a happy person.
The smell of greed from a selfish person.

No matter how far I run away
the scents of such hearts
do not leave me.

고독

나는 바닷가 모래 위에
한 개의 조개.

내 고독을 잊으라고
파도가 달려온다.

그래도 외롭다고
하늘에 새들이 날아오른다.
나는 허공에
그리운 이의 이름을 불렀다.

LONELINESS

I am a clam
on the sandy ocean beach.

The wave rushes to me
to help me forget the loneliness.

Because I'm still lonely
birds fly into the sky.
I call out into space
the name of the one I miss.

세월호에서

엄마가 마지막 남긴
전화 목소리가 나는 좋아요.

안내 방송이 들려와요
선실 안에서 가만히 있으라는 말.

엄마, 겁이나요.
물이 배 안으로 들어와요

잠시 후 선실 안은 전등이 꺼지고
물은 꽃들의 목까지 차올랐어요.
버둥거리는 물소리만
여기저기서 들려왔습니다.

엄마, 나는 살아 있어요.
죽은 세월 호에서 찾지 마세요.

ON BOARD THE FERRY SEWOL*

Mom, I love your voice
which you last left on my phone.

The PA system says
to remain calm in our cabins.

Mom, I am scared.
Water is coming in.

Shortly after, the lights went out
in the cabin and the water was filling it
up to our neck.
Only the sound of water swishing
by the bodies could be heard here and there.

Mom, I am alive.
Please do not look for me
in the dead boat Sewol.

*The overloaded ferry that capsized and sank on 16 Apr. 2014 off
South Korea, killing more than 300 passengers, mostly high school
students on a school trip. Only 172 out of 476 on board survived.

지는 꽃 옆에서

지는 꽃이 어디 그대뿐인가.
봄에 아름답게 피었던
보랏빛 자카란다 꽃도
며칠 사이로 져 버렸네.

바람은 어디나 불어오고
비는 어디나 내리는데
어떻게 피할 수 없네.

세상의 꽃이란 꽃들은
바람에 지고
비에 젖어 떨어지니

들꽃 중에도
깊이 사랑하는 그대의 손잡고
이 세상 길 가지 않을 수 없네.

WILTING FLOWERS

You are not the only flower wilting.
The purple jacaranda flowers
beautifully abloom in the spring
wilt in a few days.

The wind blows everywhere
and rain comes to everywhere, too—
how can we avoid them?

All flowers in the world
will fall in the wind
and in the rain.

Among the wild flowers,
holding hands, you whom I deeply love,
I can't help but travel this world.

종착역을 바라보며

기차는 나를 태우고 달려갑니다.
내 백발은 바람이 부는 대로 흔들리고
기차가 움직일 때마다
내 몸은 넘어지지 않으려고 긴장합니다.

기차가 종착역에 다가오고 있음을 느낍니다.
이젠 내릴 준비를 해야 되겠지요.
마지막 당신 곁을 떠나도
나는 종착역에 내려서
어딘가 당신이 올 때까지
기다리지요.

하지만 나에게 오더라도
급히 서둘러 오지 않겠다고
약속해 주겠지요.

LOOKING AT THE LAST STATION

The train I am on is running.
My grey hair is blown by the wind
and I struggle not to fall
as the train keeps moving.

I feel the train, nearing the last station.
Now I have to get ready to get off.
Even though I leave you finally
finally, I will get out of the terminal
and wait somewhere for you
until you come.

But even if you are coming to me,
promise me that you
won't hurry.

매화꽃 곁에서

가을날 붉게 타는 꽃처럼
그대를 보고 있으면
내 마음은 불덩이로 타오른다.

겨울날 눈이 내려
쌓이고 쌓여도
눈 속에서 꺾이지 않고 피는
매화꽃을 막을 수는 없다.

세상에 꽃들이
많고 많아도
그대 향한 내 사랑만큼
기쁨을 느끼지 못하네.

BY THE APRICOT BLOOMS

Like the burning red blooms on an autumn day,
when I see you
my heart burns in a fireball.

Even when weighted down
by piles of winter snow
one cannot stop
the persevering apricot blooms.

Even though there are many, many
flowers in this world
one cannot know the pleasure
of my love for you.

단풍 든 나무

푸른 잎사귀들
그 사이에서
단풍 든
잎사귀를 보았다.

하늘 높은 나뭇가지
그 파릇한 잎사귀에도
가장 낮은 나뭇가지
그 파릇한 잎사귀에도
단풍이 들리.

가을바람은 종을 치며
급하게 달려오고
잠시 소유했던
푸른 잎사귀들
하나도 남김없이
내어주겠지.
가을 나무는

AUTUMNAL TREE

Between green leaves,
I saw
a leaf
autumn-hued.

Lush leaves
of sky high boughs,
lush leaves
of the lowest boughs,
all will in autumn fall.

The autumn wind comes blowing,
its bell pealing,
and the autumnal tree
will release the green leaves
briefly in its possession,
without retaining
a single one.

하얀 민들레꽃

가을바람에 하얀 날개 달고
세상 끝까지 날아갑니다.
온갖 욕심, 강물에게 던져주고
가벼운 마음 들고 갑니다.
답답한 마음, 바다에게 던져주고
기쁜 마음 들고 갑니다.
당신 말씀, 늘 파도처럼 살아나
내 마음 출렁입니다.

당신 사랑, 내 영혼에 불을 질러
펄럭이는 감사의 깃발.
당신 눈물, 바람에 날개 달아
세상에 전하는 사랑의 꽃씨.
당신이 씨 뿌린 지난 세월들
가는 곳마다 꽃을 피우게 하신 당신입니다.

WHITE DANDELION

Tying white wings to the autumn wind
they fly to the end of the world.
Tossing out all greed to the waters of the river
they go with a light heart.
Tossing out all frustrations into the sea
they go joyously.
Your words come alive like ocean waves
and stir my mind.

Your love enkindle my soul
which flutters like a banner of gratitude.
Your tears are the seeds of love
that are delivered to the world in the wind.
In the days that have passed, you have sowed your seeds
and have made flowers bloom wherever the seeds blew.

바닷가에서

바닷가에서
나는 앞만 보고 걸었네.

시원한 바람이 불어올 때마다
밀려왔다 밀려가는 바닷물.

너무도 괴로워 슬픔을 지우려고
젖은 모래 위에 남긴 나의 발자국.

뒤를 돌아보니 아무도 보이지 않는데
나와 다른 사람의 발자국 보았네.

나와 함께 걷는 당신은
누구일까? 눈에는 보이지 않고.

AT THE BEACH

At the beach
I just walked in front.

Every time a cool breeze blows
The seawater pushed and pushed.

To get rid of sadness.
My footprints on wet sand.

Looking back, I cannot see anyone.
I saw the footprints of me and others.

You walk with me
Who is it? Invisible to the eye.

눈물

내 사랑의 눈물은
세상에서 가장 아름다운
보석.

파란 하늘과
흐르는 강물도
당신을 사랑하는 마음보다
아름답지 않네.

내 사랑은
당신을 향해 빛나는
저녁노을.

당신을 향해 흘리는
내 눈물은
눈보다 희고 꽃보다 아름답네.

TEARS

The tears of my love
are the most beautiful jewels
of the world.

The blue sky
and the river flowing by
are not as beautiful as the heart
that loves you.

My love is
the evening sunset
that glows for you.

The tears I shed for you
are whiter than snow,
more beautiful than flowers.

우리가 흔들리지 않는다면

사막에서도
눈이 내리면
무릎 꿇은 들풀들을 본다.

겨울바람이 불면
낮아지고 더 낮아지며
겨울 햇볕으로도
견디어 내는 풀뿌리.

봄바람 불어오니
무릎 꿇은 들풀들,
고요 속에서 깨어나
다시 무성한 풀숲을 이룬다.
우리가 흔들리지 않는다면

IF WE DO NOT GIVE IN

Even in the desert,
when it snows,
the grass in the field kneels down.

When the winter wind howls,
the grassroots grow deeper and deeper
and the grass perseveres in the winter sun.

When the spring breezes blow
the prostrated grass
wakes up in quietude
and builds another lush grass forest.

If it does not give in.

기러기 가족

한 기러기 가족이
하늘 높이 날아가고 있습니다.

만일 힘들거든 그냥 짐 싸서
귀가해라.

그런 약한 말 하지 마세요.
많은 개구리들이
말을 듣겠어요.

너는 한숨 쉬는 날
그날이 올지도 모르잖아.

약해지지 마세요.
우리에겐 날개가 있잖아요.

GOOSE FAMILY

A goose family is flying high
in the sky

If it's hard, just pack it up.
Return home.

Please do not say that.
You weaken your words.
Many frogs will listen

The day you sigh so deeply,
You may come that day.

Please do not weaken.
We will have wings.

진실

너는 마음의 밭에
거짓이 없는
진실의 씨앗만을 뿌리거라.

네가 거짓의 씨를 뿌려서
감추면 감출수록
벗기고 싶은 진실.

아무리 네가
양파껍질처럼 감추어도
거짓은 세상에 드러나게 된다.

THE TRUTH

In the field of your heart
No doubt
Just let's plant the seeds of truth

You have sown the seed of lies
If you hide,
The truth I want to strip.

No matter how you
Even if you hide it like an onion skin
Lies are revealed to the world.

Book Review

이 책에 수록된 시들은 자연— 나무, 별, 달, 바다, 비, 벌, 구름으로 포장되어 있다. 조윤호의 이미지는 선명하고 시는 간결하며 어휘의 낭비가 없다. 자연세계의 미세한 측면도 시인의 상상력에 불을 지르고 거기에서 얻는 통찰은 독자들을 예기치 못했던 기쁨 속으로 던져준다. "달이 미소한다."던가 "빛은 밝혀 주기를 실패한다면 빛이 아니다."라고 하는 쾌감. 먼지로부터 불꽃이 상기되고 낙엽의 그림자로부터 빛이 솟아나기도 한다. 작품들은 놀랍고, 위안이 되고, 동요시킨다. 마치 삶처럼, 때로는 길이 위안을 주고 평온하다. 때로는 소요스럽고 불안으로 가득 차 있다. 조윤호 시인은 민감한 정서의 거장임을 환기적 언어로 드러낸다. 우리의 육신을 짜릿하게 하는 울림의 언어.

—**빌 월랙** (미국시인/ 번역가)

우리는 복합적인 시대에 살고 있다. 정보의 과잉적재, 과학기술로 인한 산만, 동시 다발적인 작업 수행의 요구로 인해 집중력 미달 장애까지 일어나고 있다. 그럼으로 시집 『사랑의 빛』을 통해 조윤호 시인의 시를 접할 수 있음은 얼마나 아름다운 일인가. 시 「가을바람」에서 시인은 미묘한 상세함으로 소박한 가랑잎 하나, 빗나간 나뭇가지 하나에서 영감을 얻으며, 그 어느 때보다도 중요한 시인과 자연세계와의 관계에서 영감을 얻는다. 시 「가을 하늘엔 별이 빛나네」는 나무에서 커가는 사과와 인간 심장과의 환유적 연관을 가지며 둘이 다 '빨갛게 익어간다.' 마찬가지로 시 「소나기 소리」에서 '번개와 천둥이 치더니'는 사랑의 가망성에 설레는 시인의 모습을 보여준다. 『사랑의 빛』 시집에는 시인이 세상에서 자신의 위치를 찾으며 자연에서 배우는 교훈이 들어있다. 시 「물처럼」에서 시인은 친절을 삶의 길로 선택하며 바위를 깎아내리는 물의 우아한 흐름과 동일시하며 영혼의 이미지를 찾는다. 그리고 '부드러움이 강함을 이긴다는 것을/보여준다.' 깊은 감정의 빛이 난다. 예를 들면 「눈 위의 발자국」에서 시인이 사랑의 문 앞에서 문이 안 열리면 '아픈 발자국이 녹아서/ 강물처럼 흐르리라'고 선언한다. 감정의 풍경이 시간에 따라 이동될 때, 주의 깊게 초점에 맞추어진 시들 속에서 고체가 액체가 되고, 마침내, 아름다운 시 「눈 속에서」 사랑이 모든 것을 이겨낸다. '그러나 사랑이 우리 마음에 쌓일 때/ 무거운 눈도 가벼워진다.' 시집 『사랑의 빛』에서 조윤호 시인은 우리에게 가장 고귀한 기술을 가르쳐 준다: 진정 관심을 갖는 법.

—**마리아 베넷** (미국시인/번역가)

작가에 대하여

조윤호는 경상남도 창원에서 출생, 1963년『자유문학』신인상에 시가 당선되어 문단에 데뷔했다. 1971년 미국에 이민했고, 미국의 시전문지『Lips』와『Paterson Literary Review』, 영국 웨일즈의 시전문지『The Seventh Quarry』, 그리고 루마니아의 문예지와 폴란드 문예지에도 시를 발표했다.

그의 시집은『풀꽃처럼 만나리』,『시인나무』,『고뇌하는 당신』,『강은 마음을 비운다』,『사과나무의 사랑』등 5권이 있다.

그는 1997년「가산문학상」을 받았고, 2012년에는「미주시인협회」(현 재미시인협회) 시인상을 수상했다. 2017년에는 이탈리아 토리노의 시인단체 Immagine & Poesia (상상과 시)의 Guido Gozzano (귀도 고짜노) 기념사업회 주최 국제 시 경연대회에서 시「사랑의 빛」으로 국제부문 시문학상을 수상했다.

ABOUT THE AUTHOR

Yoon-Ho Cho was born in Changwon, Gyengsang-nam-do Province, S. Korea. He made his literary debut in 1963 by winning the New Writer's Award of the Korean *Jayu Munhak Literature.* He immigrated to the US in 1971 and has been published in numerous journals, such as the American poetry journals *Lips, The Paterson Literary Review,* and the Welsh poetry journal *The Seventh Quarry,* and *in* Romanian and Polish literary journal's.

He has published five books of poetry, including *Meet Like Wildflowers, Poet's Tree, You are agonizing, The River Empties Its Heart,* and *The Love of an Apple Tree.*

In 1997, he received the 4th Gasan Literature Award, and in2012, The Korean-American Poet Association honored him with their Literature Award. In 2017, he received the Honorable Mention for his poem "Light of Love" at the International Poetry Contest held by the poetry group Immagine & Poesia, Amici de Guido Gozzano, and Comune de Aglie.